Phrases Of You

A Poetry Collection

Jemaine Chettiar

BookLeaf Publishing

India | USA | UK

Dedication

For, Rach. The woman who birthed me. You are the blood in my veins, the feeling in my bones and the fire in my soul. The world does not deserve you, and I will remind you of this every day, for all eternity.

Preface

The words within these pages explore a mosaic of experiences that I have lived through and some that I have not. This is an ode to feeling. All feelings, good, bad and everything in between. I have spent so much time trying to understand things instead of just feeling them.

So much so, that all I have left are memories and recollections of moments that once were. Spending your thoughts living in those moments can bring a tapestry of emotions to the surface. I can never truly make you feel what I feel. The longing for understanding, the yearning to be understood. It is a disease. However, it is only human nature. So, I use my words in a lousy attempt to make you understand an unreliable translation of a language that does not exist.

Acknowledgements

I would like to express my gratitude to my mother, Rachael Murugan. Having a strong woman of God like you by my side has proven to be an advantage. And my father, Terrance Chettiar. You never say much except that you are proud of me. I never know what's going on in your head, much like my own, but you motivate me to be the best version of myself. I would like to thank my friends that have showered me with unconditional love and support (if you have to question it then it's probably not you). Knowing you believe in me is like oil in my lamp. I would also like to thank the people who have been by my side on this journey as a poet. To conclude, I would like to thank God because my faith keeps me afloat, without him I would drown.

1. Pretty boy

Teach me how to speak the language of life
Coffee rings on your page
And pen smudges on your fingers
Let's write our own story
Slip on that vintage sweater of yours
And let me dance with your silhouette
On an afternoon where the rain fogs up your glasses
Right on the corner
We can laugh in silence
As we sway into our ephemeral forever
And when you are gone
I will go back to that corner
And listen to the streets as they call your name

2.

Let us love in slow motion

Living an entire lifetime in each moment

Let us delay every action and reaction

Every touch and every caress

This way your fingers can linger a little longer in my hair

And our souls can spend a little more forever with each other.

3.

You will never be a distant memory to me
You will forever be entangled in the depths of my soul.

4. Mother

My mother never gave me gentle, quiet love that you
only hear in whispers
My mother gave me the kind of love that you scream
from rooftops
The kind of love that loves you out loud
In bold colors and fonts dancing in the sky for eternity

My mother never gave me conditional, temporary love
My mother gave me an abundance of love that you could
use to heal a broken heart that feels defeated
The kind of love that engulfs you in a blanket of
tenderness
like Earl Grey on a cold morning before leaving home

5. Red Light

This love feels misunderstood
But the way your eyes smile at me
Makes me forget that we shouldn't be holding hands
Makes me forget that I shouldn't love you at all

6. Young Warrior Woman

She wears her scares like accessories to the perfect outfit.
Her crown laden with thorns, still she reigns victorious
and courageous.
Aphrodite
She is more precious than ammolite
Venus
She knows no weakness
She does not need a knight in shining armor
For when she wields her sword, she is a hero amongst
the masses.
Hear my praises,
Young Warrior Woman.

7. Figments

A stone thrown at a window
A burning desire to kiss the girl beside you
Staring into her eyes as the incandescent light blinds
your soul
What is this hypnotic feeling
Of standing so close to you
As the world spins twice as fast on its axis
Letting me know that you're just a mirage

8.

No inhibitions,
not when I'm around your whiskey eyes.
I find it hard to complete my sentences.
Especially when I get the urge to taste your smile
And I fall into-

9.

       Kiss me on the beach in Santa Monica
Bury your face in my neck
Let us become one as you weave yourself into me
I wish to die like this

10.

One day I will write you a poem
That will reach into the depths of your soul
And shake you awake
Until you are able to see
The world in fluorescent colors
Even when your eyes are closed

11.

"Join me, my love, let us drink the life from everything",
she said.
Then she grabbed me by the collar of my shirt
And led me into the woods
With that daydream look that she wore so tragically
As the crescent moon watched over us.

12. Lona Misa

She was classical art
The kind that cannot be mastered or manipulated
The graphic quality that conceals itself like the moon
Vivid colours illuminated her eyes
And often you'd find yourself lost in their labyrinth
My chaos and my muse
Her loose brushstrokes as effortless as the stars are scattered in my midnight sky
Even in her ordinary moments I brought my easel to her
In all time
In all light I drown my paintbrush In her colour palette

13. Forever boy

You hypnotized me
With your collared shirt under your
sweater
And the way you lick your lips when
you laugh
But most of all you hypnotized me
With the way you stood in the
fractured moonlight
And gazed upon the sky like it would
be for the last time

14.

14

Our backs to the sun
A little flower stuck in your hair
My fears gripping me tightly
But your hand gripping me tighter
The fractured light blinding us both
As we became ruins
That memory seems
Like it was a moment ago
Like it was a lifetime ago
And I know well enough that I write too many poems
about you

15.

We danced in the fields of wildflowers
Not a care about the dark abyss that tomorrow held
Our hair flying as the force of the wind drew us together
The shiver in feeling your touch
Our lips arching to form crooked smiles
Oh, what ecstasy dwelled
In your asymmetrical tapestry

Clinging on to the little child that lived inside us
We ran from all the problems the world made ours to bare
The merciless rays of the golden medallion that lived in the sky against our face
A burning and blinding sensation that reminded us of what it was like to feel
What it was like to feel something real
Oh, what life dwelled in our temporary euphoria

16.

Come a little closer, love
Lay your head on the side of my pillow
May these late night memories never fade
Even when cloaked demons take control of my mind
Even when I do not recognize myself anymore.

17.

I haven't heard from you
I think you're with some other girl
The one with the rebellious smile
And the red lipstick.
I would give anything to taste her lips
Because they taste like you.

18.

Your pain should not become hate,

It should become strength.

The strength to wield a sword that defends your crown.

19.

A half-written love letter
Ink running down your fingers
As you cling to a moment that you once knew
Why can I taste the bitterness of your broken heart?

20. House Beit

Dark circles under your eyes
Your hand intertwined with mine
As the sharp cold of winter gutted us
The warmth of your smile was all I had.

21.

Don't leave me alone,
Where the only sounds I hear are echoes.
Lead me out of this labyrinth,
I will follow the crimson that stains your lips.
Don't let my demons find me,
I cannot fight long enough
For my soul to get away.